Concentration

How to Improve Concentration at Work, School, and Home

Justin Frind

Introduction

You are about to learn the key to achieving success by being more focused in everyday life! In such a hectic world, it is no wonder that we are not living our lives to the fullest.

With work, school, kids, and all of the other stresses life throws our way, how is one expected to concentrate enough to get the things they need to complete on a daily basis?

Even if you have lost all hope of regaining the concentration you need to succeed, you have stumbled upon the right place!

Within this Book, we will discuss:

- A deeper meaning into why society today has such a hard time concentrating

- The science behind attentiveness

- The importance and benefits that come along with being able to genuinely concentrate

- Strategies to hone your concentration skills for the home, work, and school

- Techniques to help folks with concentration-hindering disorders, such as ADHD, etc.

- How developing concentration techniques helped me in my everyday life to become more successful

In a world that thrives on distracting people just like you and me, no matter our levels of self-discipline, isn't it time we took back the reigns of our lives to make it the best we possibly can? You have the power to master any or all the strategies packed into this book. The power of concentration can lead you to ultimate greatness and achievement in your life. What are you waiting for?

While there might be other books on the subject that attempt to teach you the secrets to better concentration, there are none quite like this one on the market. I wrote this for readers that used to be in my own shoes, lost and headed down all the wrong paths with foggy goggles on. That's no way to walk through life! Which is why every effort was made to ensure that the Book is full of as much useful information as possible, please enjoy!

Table of Contents

Concentration in a Chaotic World.........9

Top 5 Reasons Society Is Distracted 10

Not enough exercise.......................10
Excess stress 11
Dissatisfaction with your job..........11
Lack of sleep....................................11
Overload of technology and information12

The Importance of Concentration in Life14

The Key to Success 17
Benefits of Boosting Concentration:.......17
Quotes to Open Your Eyes to the Power of Concentration 19

The Science of Concentration 21

The Brain and Concentration..................22
How We Lose Our Sense of Concentration23
How to Strategically Utilize All That Information..25

Concentration Home Remedies...........27

Lifestyle changes for enhanced concentration..28

Concentration Strategies for the Workplace..34

Tips for Regaining Focus in the Workplace 35
Concentration Strategies in the Workplace 39

- Prioritize your tasks 39
- Limit distractions 40
- Break it down into bite-sized pieces 41
- Find a quiet spot 41
- Use a timer 42
- Plan ahead 42
- Use relaxation techniques 42
- Take notes 43

Concentration Strategies to Use in School Settings 44

Concentration Strategies for Teachers ... 44
Strategies for Better Concentration in College 47

Techniques to Strengthen Concentration in All Other Aspects of Life 49

- Exercises to Strengthen Attention 49
- Increase your focus over time 50
- Make a to-do list for distractions 51
- Build-up your willpower 51
- Meditation 52
- Exercise 53
- Memorize 53
- Read slower 53
- Remain curious 54

Strategies to Better Concentration in Individuals with Concentration-Hindering Disorders 55

Deep breathing exercises 55
Background noise 56
Clean your workspace 56
Dissect tasks 56
Accountability partner 56
Repeat conversations 57
Concentrated distractions 57
Visual reminders 57

How Learning Concentration Strategies Changed My Life 58

Conclusion 61

© **Copyright 2018 by Cyberchill – Justin Frind All rights reserved.**

The following Book is reproduced below with the goal of providing information that is as accurate and as reliable as possible. Regardless, purchasing this Book can be seen as consent to the fact that both the publisher and the author of this book are in no way experts on the topics discussed within, and that any recommendations or suggestions made herein are for entertainment purposes only. Professionals should be consulted as needed before undertaking any of the action endorsed herein.

This declaration is deemed fair and valid by both the American Bar Association and the Committee of Publishers Association and is legally binding throughout the United States.

Furthermore, the transmission, duplication or reproduction of any of the following work, including precise information, will be considered an illegal act, irrespective of whether it is done electronically or in print. The legality extends to creating a secondary or tertiary copy of the work or a recorded copy and is only allowed with an expressed written consent of the Publisher. All additional rights are reserved.

The information in the following pages is broadly considered to be a truthful and accurate account of facts, and as such any inattention, use or misuse of the information in question by the reader will render any resulting actions solely under their purview. There are no scenarios in which the publisher or the original author of this work can be, in any fashion, deemed liable for any hardship or damages that may befall them after undertaking information described herein.

Additionally, the information found on the following pages is intended for informational purposes only and should thus be considered, universal. As befitting its nature, the information presented is without assurance regarding its continued validity or interim quality. Trademarks are mentioned without written consent and can in no way be considered an endorsement from the trademark holder.

Concentration in a Chaotic World

From wavering between getting work done and checking social media, to daydreaming about a better life, losing your keys and everything in-between, life is hectic in this day and age. In today's world, we are expected to multitask, juggle jobs, families, the home, and fulfill many other obligations. All seems easy enough, but we fail at remaining focused and staying alert, especially when we need to the most.

If I had to give a description of our generation and list the reasons why we are so distracted today as a society, they would have to be:

- **Lack of ability to focus**

- **The drastic changes in gender and cultural roles**

- **Too many options to choose from**

It is hard to focus. How many times today have you checked your phone for emails, texts, and social media notifications?

Many of us find it daunting to concentrate. I know before I challenged myself to become a more focused individual, I always felt like I had been on a stair machine all day. I felt fuzzy, as if my brain was in a constant fog, with it being difficult to bring things to the surface that I did know. I soon realized that my lack of focus was the one thing in common when it came to not being able to move forward in life.

If you think about it, the ability to focus is seen as a superpower rather than an everyday life skill. If you can sit down and work on something without becoming distracted, many people would say you have a 'rare skill.' When did our world become this?

Top 5 Reasons Society Is Distracted

There are lots of reasons we lose focus in everyday life, and the five things listed below suck our attentiveness away the most.

Not enough exercise

By exercising on a regular basis, it allows our mind to stay sharp and increases our overall learning capacity, expanding our memory capabilities. Sweating as a result of exercise helps you burn off excess energy that may cause you to become fidgety, which can help you to sleep better and maintain focus.

Excess stress

Stress is detrimental to concentration because it competes with your cognitive centers, which are responsible for creating sharp, quick thoughts. Anxiety drags our focus down further. This is why meditation, which is one of the strategies we will talk about later in this book, is beneficial. It is an exercise that improves our attention span and relieves us from depression and anxiety symptoms.

Dissatisfaction with your job

Being unhappy at your place of work from time to time is inevitable, especially when you got poor feedback or if a presentation flopped. Disorganized workspaces and boring projects are normal reasons for our focus to become foggy in the workplace. But, if you find yourself always running behind on getting projects done and missing deadlines, then concentration is something that you need to focus on.

Lack of sleep

If you fail to get a good amount of sleep each evening, your body and mind become irritable as it is trying to deal with major mind fog, which makes it almost impossible to manage everyday tasks. Adequate rest is key when it comes to concentration.

Overload of technology and information

All of us have more than just one technological device we use on a daily basis. From computers, laptops, mobile phones, tablets, MP3 players, etc., these devices are all competing for our attention. Our brains are capable of acting as a type of secretary, helping us to manage time and remain organized. However, we have taught ourselves to excessively multitask, which makes it much more difficult to remain focused on a singular task.

The biggest reason why currently our attention span is comparable to that of a fish (perhaps worse at times) is that of the hyperactive world that we are forced to dwell in. The procreation of content is a means for the creation of chaos. We witness an overload of data each day, which makes us crave instant gratification, even more, decreasing our overall ability to focus.

Our contemporary society does not favor the same things our ancestors did during the times of human evolution. Natural selection no longer kills the individuals that don't pay as much attention. This means that we will continuously be fighting against maintaining our focus for accomplishment against the new, latest technological trends unless we start to do something about it in our personal and professional lives.

The good news? It is possible to channel our attention to more meaningful things that do not put us at risk of death. I am sure as you are reading this, you realize that you have always wanted to increase your self-control within our society's era of endless information, which makes you even more human than our ancestors. If we can put our highest faculties on top of our priority list, we gain back our free will.

The Importance of Concentration in Life

Before we dive into strategies that you can start utilizing in your day-to-day life to increase your levels of concentration, you need to genuinely realize the power that concentration has over your life.

The ability to remain focused, even when the world is fighting for our attention, is one of the essential capabilities you can possess, especially in a society where concentration is highly lacking. The attention of people wanders off into oblivion without the ability to reel it back to one topic.

Concentration is the skill to focus on a single thought or topic while eliminating all else from your conscious mind and awareness. Trained minds can focus without becoming distracted by outside sources, noises, or inner thoughts and feelings.

So, why is it vital to be able to possess the power to focus your mind? Because it is a skill that helps you in all aspects of life, from driving, working, reading, studying, completing tasks, meditating, and everything in-between.

Concentrating helps you to:

- Strengthen intuition
- Hone meditation skills
- Work more productively
- Conserve energy for essential tasks
- Improve study skills
- Improve overall memory
- Frees the mind from pestering thoughts
- Retrieve a sense of inner peace
- Controls thoughts and feelings

I like to tell my readers to compare your level of concentration to that of a light bulb, the rays from the bulb scatters in all directions, spreading the energy. Even if you are standing several feet away, you can see the light but cannot feel the heat. Your mind works in the same way. Our brains think of many things, one after the other, without thinking too much on the depth of a topic in particular. Average minds don't utilize their power to its full potential.

Think about the development and creation of the laser, it takes rays of light and lines it up into a single source. They vibrate when in harmony and is much greater than that of the concentration of a light bulb, even from many feet away. The laser has the power to go right through your body. The light bulb is ordinary light, while the laser is a perfect depiction of the power of concentrated light.

Concentrated thoughts have greater power since its power lies within the heightened perception possessed by people who can see more of the truths that lie beneath life's phenomena. Concentrated minds are also relaxed minds. When a practiced, concentrated person becomes engrossed in a subject, their brains and bodies become relaxed as they absorb that topic's knowledge.

Despite popular belief, concentration is essential for pretty much everything in life. It prevents us from wandering in all directions aimlessly. Without a form of attentiveness, we would be unable to complete anything. If you don't believe me, look around you. The work of concentrated minds is more enjoyable, and they can do all sorts of work in highly productive ways.

Those that cannot concentrate make much more mistakes and take a long time to complete things, if they ever get them done at all. They will continue to think and perform things at a slow pace, which results in excess worry and poor application of actions.

The Key to Success

On all levels of activity that is mentally done, concentration can be seen as the key to succeeding. Concentrated minds allow people to solve issues readily and can attract opportunities for success.

Those with a concentrated mindset see inspirations in their work and thinking. It allows mental powers and channels to awaken the mind, which erases obstacles and brings about great insights.

Benefits of Boosting Concentration:

- Greater sense of willpower

- Ability to make quick decisions

- Choosing your own thoughts instead of allowing the mind to wander

- Provides us with the inner strength to make decisions that eventually lead to success

- Better focus

- Boost both short and long-term memory

- A heightened sense of self-confidence

- Better meditation practices

- A better sense of inner contentment

- Freedom from annoying thoughts that distract you

- Ultimate peace of mind (what everyone desires)

- Better control of thoughts and emotions

Quotes to Open Your Eyes to the Power of Concentration

Not convinced about the power that concentration has on your overall life? Then I am sure the following quotes from these successful individuals throughout history might just change your mind for the better.

- *"The jack of all trades seldom is good at any. Concentrate all of your efforts on one definite chief aim."*
  — **Napoleon Hill**

- *"It's shocking how little there is to do with tennis when you're just thinking about nothing except winning every point."*
  —**Andre Agassi**

- *"The secret to success in any human endeavor is total concentration."* — **Kurt Vonnegut Jr.**

- *"When I am away, I am with it. When I am with it, I am away."*
  —**Aditya Ajmera**

- *"Success is like a camera. Only focus on what is most important. Ignore trivial details. Concentrate on your main goal image for success. Develop your picture. If they don't turn out, don't give up. Take more shots at it. Always be persistent. Focus on making success clearly happen."*
  —Mark LaMoure

- *"If our thoughts and hopes are elsewhere, it is impossible to set out faces steadily toward the work required of us."*
  —Anonymous

The Science of Concentration

Concentration is the skill that gives us the power to direct every single one of our physical and mental capabilities to one objective and prevents us from becoming distracted or confused.

The problem is that our senses are constantly bombarded with multiple streams of information, from the light coming in the window, to the sounds of the streets outdoors, the words of conversations happening in the apartment next to ours, dogs barking in the background, kids trying to gain our attention, the feeling we get when our elbows rub against a table, etc. Every time we take notice of something new in the environment we are in, we pay immediate attention to it. This is where the skill of selective attention comes in handy.

Thanks to selective attention, we can get things done. It enables us to remain focused on things without becoming distracted by things in our immediate environment, our thoughts, or our emotions. It causes other aspects of our life to literally fade into the background and helps us to refocus our attention on the task at hand if we do get caught off guard with distractions.

The Brain and Concentration

There are two regions of the brain that are responsible for controlling attention and concentration: the frontal lobe and the parietal cortex. Those are the parts of your mind you can thank for that awesome feeling of becoming engrossed in collaborations with your mind to achieve goals and get tasks done as you blur the rest of the world around you. They are responsible for finding your rhythm and sweet spot when it comes to those work-induced trances.

- → The **prefrontal cortex** helps to induce the power of willful concentration. The neurons within this region create impulses at gradual frequencies to help control voluntary actions to attention.

- → The **parietal cortex** helps to activate automatic attention. This was especially true for our ancestors when riveting sounds, such as the attack of animal, activated this portion of the brain. The neurons in this cortex create pulses of electricity at quicker rates to enable the processing of automatic attention.

The truth is, every single one of us battles to sustain concentration in everyday life. We face a plethora of distractions that keep our minds from remaining tuned into one task. It is vital to grasp what is actually happening in the brain when you are focused compared to when you get distracted.

To be able to really focus on things while blurring out other things that compete for our attention is the exact definition of selective attention. The thing is, we could focus on anything when we have the desire to.

How We Lose Our Sense of Concentration

Did you know the core of losing your ability to focus is actually evolutionary? It is a system that requires concentration to break down when a situation turns out to be risky or rewarding. This breaking down of concentration was meant to keep us safe since it is ultimately controlled by an involuntary attention system. You have no control over it, for it is hard-wired in your brain in a passive manner.

Three of the most common stimuli that break our focus are bright flashing lights, bright flashing colors, and loud sounds. Bright and novel flashes are meant to win the brain's attention. Known as gamma waves, these can have trouble getting through to your brain in loud surroundings.

Once you have your focus broken, it could take up to half an hour to return back to that original level of concentration. We can only maintain focus around fifty percent of the time. During the workday, an average employee is interrupted every three to ten minutes, from co-workers, phone calls, emails, etc. But, our brains can focus on something in particular for two hours at first, which then requires a 20 to 30-minute break to get back into the rhythm of that concentration.

If you want someone to blame for your natural inability to not focus up to your potential attention levels, then you can point right at multitasking. We have been taught to multitask from a young age. Our minds become so busy with doing a bunch of things all at once that it is challenging to transition to focus on one thing at a time.

The harsh reality is, our brain cannot process more than one aspect of information at a time effectively. Those that only lightly multitask are better able to organize their memories when switching back and forth between tasks. When we put ourselves in situations where more than one source of information is coming at us, we are not able to filter between relevant and irrelevant information fast enough. The failure to filter is what affects our ability to concentrate thanks to the brain being bogged down by all that irrelevant information.

How to Strategically Utilize All That Information

With all the information that bombards our lives, how in the world does one start to improve their overall levels of concentration?

First, I want you to see your brain as plastic. This means that our cognitive abilities can result in a better and longer attention span. You must learn how to mentally connect to the task at hand and understand the real reason why you are completing it in the first place. For instance, if you are completing a business project, recall why it is important that you should do well on it.

To keep outside factors from stealing away your attention, you will need to do whatever you can to block out those distractions. My favorite way is by listening to music, which keeps out any of those pesky outside noises. When you listen to the same album, your brain becomes accustomed to those rhythms, which will help your brain to block out everything in the background except that task.

Now that you understand the basics of the way our minds utilize concentration in everyday life, I am sure you are ready to get to the good stuff! Learning tried and true strategies to enable you to stay focused, no matter what distractions attempt to get in your way!

Concentration Home Remedies

If you find yourself being forgetful often, like forgetting appointments, not remembering tiny errands, or remembering names, then do I have a treat for you! No, this does not mean you have ADHD by the way, which many adults tend to believe when they get distracted and fail to accomplish anything.

Besides the ever-increasing levels of distractions in our everyday world, our society is majorly sufficient in deficiencies that create a negative impact on our overall concentration and our capabilities with memory.

No worries, though. With a combination of home remedies and lifestyle changes, you can improve your powers of concentration more than ten-fold! This chapter will reveal some of the superfoods that you may already have in your kitchen cupboards that with consumption, can make your mind an even more powerful device to achieve success.

Lifestyle changes for enhanced concentration

Before I reveal the superfoods that enhance your overall attentiveness, there are some changes you really should consider making in your everyday life if you find that a lack of concentration is what's keeping you from accomplishing your goals.

If you are a smoker or a heavy drinker of alcoholic beverages, then you need to do your best to give up smoking and chewing tobacco, since tobacco has a significant impact on the power your brain has. Along with that, alcohol does nothing but dull the brain, so make sure to limit your intake of alcoholic drinks.

Learn the concept of proper breathing techniques and meditation practices, for they help to relieve stress and keep your mind from becoming too busy and being overwhelmed with outside elements.

If you tend to be a couch potato or work a job where you are mainly sedentary, then you need to start incorporating exercise into your daily schedule. This improves your overall circulation of blood and supplies plenty of oxygen to the brain, which automatically results in memory power. With these quick lifestyle changes, you can improve your memory and concentration skills right away, and the best part is with practice, you will create a brand-new lifestyle from the changes of these habits.

If that wasn't enough to change your mind, now we will dive into the list of tasty superfoods that will help you feel younger, feel better, and boost overall confidence!
Superfoods to Boost Concentration

→ **Almonds**
    o Rich in antioxidants and omega-6 fatty acids
    o Rich in vitamins E and B6

Soak a handful of almonds in milk overnight and grind them in your morning smoothie or Add almonds to ice cream and smoothies

- **Flax Seeds**
    - Great source of omega-3 fatty acids

    Place a tablespoon of ground flaxseed to your salad
    -
    Massage your scalp with flax seed oil twice a week

- **Fish Oil**
    - Rich in omega-3 fatty acids

    Devour herring fish, salmon, sardines
    -
    Take fish oil capsules

- **Blueberries**
    - Reduces stress
    - Loaded with antioxidants
    - Improves cognitive learning and making decisions

    Consume as is or make it into a juice or smoothie

→ **Walnuts**
- Rich in omega-3
- Improves circulation of blood to the brain
- Helps to maintain great cardiovascular health
- Improves memory
- Better concentration
- Loaded with vitamin E, which slows down the aging process

Eat a nice handful of walnuts each morning with breakfast

→ **Dates**
- Loaded with vitamins and minerals like copper, potassium, phosphorus, manganese, magnesium, calcium, sulfur, and fiber
- Prevent inflammation and infection
- Improves blood flow to brain cells

Eat 4 to 5 dates per day while they are in season

-

Soak dates in overnight in milk. Grind them the following morning to consume in smoothies or as is

→ **Ginkgo Biloba**
- o Helps cognitive ability.
- o Improves blood flow throughout the body.

Consume 40 to 100 milligrams per day to improve memory and concentration

→ **Avocado**
- o Known as the 'complete food' since it contains both nutrients and healthy fat
- o Rich in potassium and omega-3 fatty acids

Mash avocado and spread on bread

-

Make an avocado smoothie or juice

-

Chop avocado and toss into salad

- **Beet Roots**
    - Rich in iron and other essential vitamins and minerals
    - Loaded with nitrites that open up blood vessels to improve blood supply to the brain

    Cook beetroots with other veggies to enhance entrees

    -

    Make beetroot juice and add to smoothies and drinks

    -

    Chop up and add to salads

- **Water**
    - Improves hydration, which leads to enhanced concentration

    Drink 8 to ten or more glasses of water per day to maintain a healthy mind

Concentration Strategies for the Workplace

Studies have shown that distractions take away a little over two hours from each workday for the average employee. And employees can only work an average of eleven minutes before getting frenzied with other things, and it takes them 25 minutes or more to get back to the task at hand.

So, what is it that is distracting us from being more productive at work? A major reason is the layout of the workplace. Open offices allow for distraction from other employees and outside sources. These type of workplace strategies that are meant to optimize productivity actually decrease effectiveness instead. With the ability to hear noise, it allows us to become distracted with co-workers walking around, chatting, and other stimuli that keep us from our work.

Social media is the next biggest disadvantage against productivity in the workplace. As a society today, we thrive in the need to socialize using countless social media platforms. Ten minutes can easily become an hour or more as employees spend their time on these applications, allowing our minds to wander far from the idea of finishing our tasks. This then causes major lapses in attention spans that end up hurting overall productivity.

Tips for Regaining Focus in the Workplace

There is no possible way for a person to focus on everything in their surroundings and somehow finish their work. Thankfully, there are a few easy to implement tips that anyone can start to use in their daily lives beginning today to heighten their overall productivity!

- If you feel like you're starting to glaze over, taking a break can help your mind to rest for a few minutes. Stand up, stretch, drink some water, have a small snack, and then sit back down. You will be surprised at how much of a pick-me-up this is!

    Tip: If you are someone that's easy prey to workplace distractions during breaks, keep a bottle of water and small snacks close to you, so you don't lead yourself to stray off course when taking a much-needed break.

- When you feel yourself losing the focus you need to perform your required tasks, simply close your eyes and sit back in your chair for a moment. This helps you to restore your focus and allows you to think for a moment, which can provide you with a new direction in your work.

- Our brains are created with a built-in braking system, located in our left prefrontal cortex. You can train your brain to be more attentive by being mindful and practicing mindful meditation. This helps you to stay concentrated when you catch your mind wandering off to far-away places. It gives you the power to bring your thoughts back to reality.

- If you are one that finds themselves tempted to check their mobile devices for notifications, just turn off those devices. Try this for just one hour, and you may surprise yourself at how much you can accomplish!

    Tip: Schedule specific times during the workday for social media and emails. Allot 15 minutes in the morning and 15 to 30 minutes in the afternoon to go through your emails and media accounts. Once you make this a habit, you will find yourself more mentally freed.

- Our bodies have a built-in wake and sleep times, as well as a circadian rhythm, which is what helps us to plan our daily activities and allow us to get the most out of the day ahead. This means discovering the most productive times of the day for you to the most optimum time to send out business tweets.

    There have been many studies that prove that people work the best before lunch. But for others, this is the worst time to work. You need to find what personally is the best for you and your schedule so that you can be the most productive. This means for both home and work life. As you plan around this rhythm, pay attention to it and use it to your full advantage.

- It's no secret that being organized provides advanced optimization when it comes to concentrating on getting things done during the workday. Put away things that you don't need right away or that will distract you later.

    Tip: Arrange items on your desk so you can get to them easily when needed.

By implementing just one or two of these easy tips into your workplace routine, you will almost immediately start to see the difference in your overall productivity as your motivation and willpower to finish your job and complete your duties increases. You can also think of and use your own strategies that work for you and your schedule. What would work better for you to make the most from your workplace environment?

Concentration Strategies in the Workplace

Don't beat yourself up if you are not getting as much done as you should be while at work. The world today makes it very difficult to get everything done during the day. But, I assure you that with these strategies, you will start making deadlines and feeling more achieved while at work.

Prioritize your tasks

This is one of the essential concentration improvements you can make starting today. Tackle the biggest things on your list first and leave the small to-do's for later in the day. No matter if you work in an office environment, or if you work from home, make it a priority to make a list of the tasks at hand for the day.

- Include everything on list 'A' that needs to be done by the end of the day or the next day.

- On list 'B,' write down projects due next week.

- On list 'C' jot out tasks that can be considered as loose ends, such as checking emails, etc.

When you prioritize tasks, this can help you to remain organized and keep distractions at bay.
Organize emails
Even if you consider yourself a focused employee, it doesn't take much to get distracted by the noises of incoming emails and other notifications. If you are prone to distractions, these types of notifications can literally derail your entire workday.

Instead of reading emails and notifications that come in throughout the day as they arrive, set a specific time that you can focus on doing this task. This helps you to remain free from being shackled by all these notifications.

Limit distractions

From casual chats outside your door to 24-hour availability on the internet to consistent voicemails coming in, there are a plethora of distractions that can drive you down an entirely different path than getting work completed. Just like emails, you need to create a particular time to check voicemails, surf the web, and have conversations with co-workers.

- Personally, I find it beneficial to shut off my computer and phone, shut my door and turn off my phone for specific periods of time.

- Declutter your workspace so that you are not spending time cleaning up and getting frustrated with clutter.

Break it down into bite-sized pieces

If you find that you often feel overwhelmed at work, break down large tasks into small, more manageable chunks. This alleviates stress and allows more room for focus. Remember to set goals that are realistic. Think one hour or one day at a time instead of focusing too much on the future.

Find a quiet spot

If only everyone could have a private office with a door that eliminates sounds, right? If you are stuck with an open office, there are ways to create a nice quiet space to do your work.

- Share your space with a co-worker? Opt for someone that does more computer than phone work. Ask them to have meetings in other areas.

- If your workspace is still too noisy to concentrate, you may want to think about doing a bundle of work at the library, home office, Starbucks, etc. When you find a comfortable place to work, this increases the natural tendency to do work.

Use a timer

I have used the timer method, and it works wonders. Simply set a timer to go off at specific intervals. This allows your mind to wander right back to the task at hand. If you are not doing a task, the timer reminds you to get back to work after a break.

Plan ahead

Many people, including myself, find it more productive when using a planner or an electronic assistant. This helps to remind you of the little things to ensure you are always prepared and meeting required deadlines.

Use relaxation techniques

When stressed at the workplace, remember it's essential to take breaks to do deep breathing, meditation, or visualization exercises. This allows you to refocus your concentration and get a sense of realization that everything you might be stressing about is not urgent. It allows you time to reassess.

Take notes

While this seems humorously old-school, taking notes during meetings and phone calls helps you to remember important details later on. It also allows you to put those details on the appropriate list and prioritize them accordingly.

Concentration Strategies to Use in School Settings

Just like their parents in a highly advanced world, kids these days do not have the attention span they used to in school thanks to increased exposure to information and entertainment via mobile devices. As a teacher today, you need to be prepared to gain and harbor those decreasing attention spans!

Concentration Strategies for Teachers

- When you plan lessons, break them down into smaller chunks. Plan 'gear shifts' in-between your lessons. They can be as simple as pairing students up with another peer to work, writing, sharing, etc. This can help students stay attentive longer since the lesson is essentially in a series of steps.

- Plan out 'brain breaks' throughout the day and make them an everyday class routine. You can go **here** for some great ideas!

- Just like it's difficult for adults to work in disorganized, messy offices, students find it hard to concentrate with bunches of bright displays and an overload of things in a classroom. Consider the visual environment and instead of rainbows and flora displays, put up informative posters for them to rest their eyes on.

- When you have students that are avoiding their work, ask them to rate the task from one to ten. If they say an eight or higher, ask them what they think could be done differently to make it to a two or three.

- Make mindfulness practice a routine in your classroom. Just 5 to 10 minutes per day can greatly improve concentration.

- Create flexible seating within your class. This is a more proactive idea to improve the way your students pay attention and learn. Traditional classrooms aim for rows of desks facing towards the front. Instead, give your students a nice variety of options so they can choose what is comfortable for them.

- Make memory games a routine in the class. These games are a simple way to get them to focus for a longer period of time, and it is a great way to instill information they have just learned.

- Ensure that you have 'fast-finisher activities' for students to do once they have completed their required work.

- Moving the body is not only a good choice for overall physical health, but it's essential for mental clarity too. Get your students up and moving, especially when they seem dull and drowsy.

Strategies for Better Concentration in College

As I was once a college student myself, I clearly remember having periods of terribly low concentration, and it drastically affected my studies. In college, many distractions can take students from their work, from suitemates, phones, music, residential halls and many more. But even students that don't live on campus face distractions at home too. Both on and off-campus students will benefit from these concentration techniques!

- Isolate yourself from becoming distracted by finding a comfortable and quiet place to study. This helps you to maintain the commitment to the task at hand.

- Your best concentration happens when you are relaxed, and your brain is fresh, so perform the hardest tasks first. This may include long reading, hard math problems, or other complex homework. Save more enjoyable tasks for later, when you have grown a bit tired, and your concentration is no longer at optimum levels.

If you know you become distracted easily, know what kinds of situations to avoid when you have work to do:

- → Place yourself in front of the class
- → Sit with other students who are focused
- → Get plenty of rest and eat a balanced meal to stay alert
- → Relate subjects that you find not interesting with something that has impacted your life. Connections keep you focused.

Get into the routine of using active techniques to study:

- → Do not study in your bed
- → Use a highlighter when you read notes and textbooks
- → Create charts, drawings, diagrams, and/or flashcards
- → Tape your notes and listen to them while you walk, drive, or exercise

Techniques to Strengthen Concentration in All Other Aspects of Life

The power of concentration not only lies in being attentive to a single task, but it is also made up of several elements that one must learn to manage to master concentration.

I like to refer to our mind as another muscle in our body. You must think this way if you wish to build your attentive muscle. Both your physical muscles and your attention 'muscles' have only limited strength, but you can make them more powerful in many ways.

The reality is, making your mental muscles stronger is all about getting nitty-gritty with old-fashioned work. It also involves fueling your body positively, getting good, quality sleep and engaging yourself in challenging exercises throughout the day.

Exercises to Strengthen Attention

Just like how you cannot grow physical muscles by being a couch potato, you will never gain strength mentally if you just sit and binge-watch Netflix all day and scroll through your social media feeds. The muscles of your mind need resistance too. They require challenges to help them stretch their limits to grow more focus fibers. Here are some exercises you can use to beef up your attention span and begin lifting heavier cognitive loads!

Increase your focus over time

Just like when you finally decide you want to get into better shape physically, you have to start from zero and work your way up. The last thing you want to do is throw yourself to the wolves by taking an intense training program. You will quit before you even begin.

If your focus is shabby, then you need to build it up slowly. I personally grew from using the 'Pomodoro Method,' which requires ones to work for 45 minutes straight and then take a 15-minute break. When you are just beginning, 45 minutes can seem like you just ran a marathon. Nevertheless, don't give up!

Set an easy goal for yourself and achieve it. For instance, set a 5-minute timer and focus on your work. Then, take a short 2-minute break before doing another 5 minutes. Keep adding time each day, and by day 9, you should be able to work 45 minutes before you need a break.

Make a to-do list for distractions

Thanks to the internet, access to trillions of websites with valuable and not so valuable information is right at our fingertips, which makes for a major distraction all on its own. We tend to let our minds wander and let it think, "Oh hey, what's new today?"

Once we get distracted, however, it is hard to return back to the tasks at hand. Plus, shifting our attentiveness back and forth throughout the day wears our energy supply down.

So, to stay on the task until completion, whenever you get the urge to check on a notification, just write it down on a piece of paper close to you. Then promise yourself that you will be able to look at it once you are done with what is in front of you first. This sounds way too simple to work but trust me, it does wonders!

Build-up your willpower

Willpower and the attention you use voluntarily are intertwined. Willpower is basically the power to ignore things that get us off tasks while staying focused. The more you practice positive willpower, the better your attentiveness will be naturally.

Meditation

Meditation was one of the best things I ever practiced since I started it back a few years ago. It keeps me calm and collected, and it has boosted my attention span ten-fold! No, you do not have to spend monstrous amounts of time meditating. Just ten to twenty minutes a day does plenty of wonders for the mind. Just after four days, I saw drastic improvements in my overall concentration.

If you need to buckle down and focus on something for a long period of time, start off the morning by focusing on your breathing and meditating for a few minutes.

In addition to that 10 to 20 minutes of meditation per day, I also highly recommend practicing mindfulness meditation as well. Mindfulness allows one to focus in on what they are doing by slowing down and taking in all the emotional and physical sensations they are experiencing at that moment in time.

You can do this while you eat, for instance. Take the time to carefully chew your food and focus on all the textures and the sensations of its flavor. While you are shaving, smell the shaving cream, feel the pleasure of the warm lather and slowly drag the razor. When you incorporate these tiny sessions of being mindful throughout the day, you will expand your attention for the times when it counts the most.

Exercise

As you have read multiple times, exercising the body and mind is very beneficial in a plethora of ways, especially when it comes to concentration. The more you engage in physical activity, the longer your span of attention becomes. Exercise has been proven to assist our minds in avoiding distractions that arise.

Memorize

Memorization games and memorizing stuff, in general, is a fantastic way to exercise your mind muscles. Memorize poems or scriptures each week. This trains your brain to improve overall memory and makes it more mentally agile.

Read slower

With advancements in smartphones, tablets, and e-readers at our fingertips, you would think we would be more avid readers, right?

Quite the opposite actually. Only around 5-percent of readers actually finish online articles and 38-percent only scroll and skim through the first few paragraphs of information.

This is a shame since complex ideas cannot be condensed down into singular paragraphs or poems. I challenge you to start reading each night before bed. This means to read slowly and really dig into the words. Also, make an effort to read a couple of longer articles during the week.

Remain curious

When we remain curious about the world around us, we have greater stamina in terms of our concentration levels.

Strategies to Better Concentration in Individuals with Concentration-Hindering Disorders

While a wandering mind is common for all of us on occasion, imagine living with a mental disorder that you literally have to fight for your life against distractions. Those with Attention Deficit Hyperactivity Disorder (ADHD), for example, this is the reality of every day. They always miss details and make plenty of mistakes. The lack of ability to focus is a prominent symptom of this disease, but there are many tips that people with this disorder can act upon to sustain their concentration and help them succeed in everyday life.

Deep breathing exercises

For those with and without ADHD alike, you would be surprised at how simple breathing exercises can aid in sustaining concentration when you are stressed. Deep breathing improves your ability to focus, for it allows blood to flow to areas of the brain that make higher decisions. When you are relaxed, your brain can function much easier.

Background noise

Having some sort of music playing in the background while you are attempting to focus tends to drown out other distractions. Turn on your ceiling fan, get out a noise-making machine, or just keep the music playing at a lower volume.

Clean your workspace

Having clutter in and around your workspace impairs the focus of even highly disciplined individuals. Clear all that clutter from your work area before attempting a project.

Dissect tasks

When projects are daunting, it is hard to focus on them. Instead, break them into pieces, step-by-step. When you make them into easy, manageable goals to achieve, you can get to work faster and stay focused longer.

Accountability partner

Ask for the support of someone you trust, whether it be a friend, member of the family, or ADHD coach. When you make a deal with someone to complete something, you feel more obligated to do it.

Repeat conversations

When you paraphrase what someone just told you, it allows your mind time to digest the information, and this ensures that you understood and grasped what they said.

Concentrated distractions

When you are sitting in a meeting at work with a boring lecturer, fiddle with something quietly, such as a pin or a stress ball. This keeps your mind from wandering and allows you to have something at your fingertips to feel the sensation of.

Visual reminders

You can use these for both short and long-term goals. When you have something tangible to connect you to objectives, you are more likely to get them done. For example, keep a piece of paper with your graduation date where you will see it often.

How Learning Concentration Strategies Changed My Life

It wasn't so long ago that I was allowing life to slide by me. I was working dead-end jobs, going to college but not really learning much, and I went to bed each evening wondering what my purpose in the world really was.

It wasn't until after I graduated college and realized the journalism degree I received was a slight bust in the world of western Kansas. I came to the realization that I not only needed to find a better calling, but I had to have the willpower and concentration to finish through with something for once in my young life!

Despite the bad rap the internet receives, when utilized in better and more positive ways, the internet is essentially what pulled me from the rabbit hole and got me to where I am today. But the internet could not do all the heavy lifting for me. When I started my journey working from home, I figured it would be easy as pie, not having to set a schedule, being able to scroll through social media when I wanted, and leaving the house whenever I could. Boy, was I mistaken.

I quickly learned the value of making a schedule and sticking to it, especially regarding the home-based business I was creating. There were many distractions I had to learn how to avoid, from my partner asking me to go out after work to my friends randomly stopping by and interrupting my workflow, etc. I am thankful that I realized early on in my work-from-home career that I had to show up for myself if I wanted my business to succeed.

While I had the schedule down pat, it was difficult not to check my phone, look at emails, and remain inside for periods of time while the sun was shining oh so brightly. This was when I learned the power of concentration techniques and exercises. I began using the techniques you have read in this book each day until I made them a habit. Now I have no idea what my life would be without morning meditations, jotting things down, creating mind games for myself, and setting timers to ensure that I get the most out of my brain power for the day.

I can easily say that without some self-discipline and concentration habits engraved in my life that I would not be the successful freelancer I am today. With a schedule intact, and the ability to keep myself shielded from pesky distractions, I have managed to totally erase the idea of having to work a 9 to 5 job and become my very own boss.

That being said, anyone can become a master at concentration, no matter if you have a mental disorder keeping you from your dreams or just plain confusion in where to start paving your path for a prosperous life.

I wish you all the best of luck in discovering a better version of yourself when it comes to what you can really accomplish when being a more focused individual.

Conclusion

I want to congratulate you for making it through to the end of *Concentration: How to Improve Concentration at Work, School, and Home*!

I first want to say thank you again for choosing to purchase this eBook to better your concentration in all aspects of everyday life. Being more attentive and observant of the world around us is a skill that is not honed by many, so give yourself a pat on the back for taking the initial step to becoming a better person!

Besides becoming a better person all the way around, you have read and learned about strategies and assortments of techniques that not many people are aware of so they can grasp the success they want out of life. Who knew that hunkering down and polishing your brain's assembly of aggregation could get you to unimaginable places? I know I personally had no idea of the power concentration had in my life until I began the journey myself with the very techniques discussed in the chapters you just absorbed.

So, on a scale of one to ten (and be honest!) how concentrated were you while reading or skimming the information of this book? Did you find yourself having to turn back pages to better grasp certain portions? Or did you manage to blur out entire chapters? No judgment if you did! I used to do the same thing! But this goes to show how concentration can ultimately change your life, starting off in small but significant ways!

The next step is to start with one to two strategies in this book; begin utilizing them and mastering them in everyday scenarios. Trust me, you will be surprised at how the tiniest of actions can impact your day for the better!

Made in the USA
Middletown, DE
10 August 2019